THE JOY OF STUFFED PREPPIES

Randall C. Douglas III — Illustrations by Eric Fowler

THE JOY OF STUFFED PREPPIES

HOLT, RINEHART AND WINSTON · NEW YORK

An Owl Book

Library of Congress Catalog Card Number: 81-48388
ISBN 0-03-061596-8
First Edition

Designer: Amy Hill
Printed in the United States of America
1   3   5   7   9   10   8   6   4   2

ISBN 0-03-061596-8

FOREWORD

Originality is not preppy. Imitation is. After years of Andover and Princeton, summers in Edgartown and winters in Hobe Sound, I know full well the virtues of following in well-worn footsteps, particularly those made by treadless Top-Siders. So if you hear echoes of one or another handbook within these pages, it's not coincidental. We are only practicing the fine points of preppyness; we know the perfect specimens we have become. But alas, we won't live forever, and no one has yet bothered to tell us what is to be done with ex-preps.

As it turns out, preppies are more useful in the past tense than in the present. This is not precisely a how-to book, but I hope you'll find in it some practical ideas for utilizing friends and acquaintances who have fizzled out. Although names and institutions have been changed to protect the unsuspecting, I hasten to add that my suggestions here are all rooted in my own experiences. I have, in fact, witnessed variations on each and every situation depicted in this book.

Do remember: To die is not preppy. To be stuffed is.

RCD III

One might think this an undignified pose for Preston Pierrepont, Jr., once the life of every party his parents threw. But on one particularly animated evening, Jr. perished after passing out in a pitcher of Bloodies, and Daddy repositioned him before rigor mortis set in. He proved a fabulous conversation piece and for the first time was able to hold his liquor.

It is the habit of those up for the weekend to pull up to the paddock and pull down a tailgate. Silent witness to this particular presteeplechase picnic is Kit Doran, whose breathing apparatus was irreparably impaired by a perversely struck polo ball. Now known fondly as the South Gate, Kit had never before swung both ways.

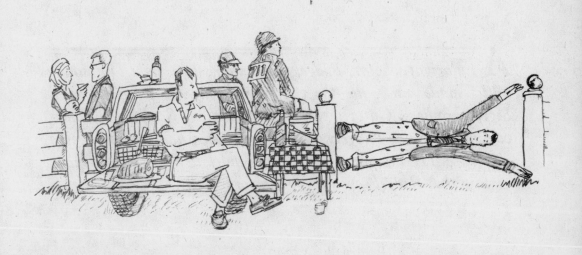

A Fulbright scholar, Ridgely Farquhar's late night lampshade antics made him quite the celebrity among his Kappa Kappa Sigma brothers. Gatoring through a puddle of Schlitz one homecoming weekend, Ridgely was done in when he wriggled over a live wire. His imaginative pals were quick to find a way to make certain that Ridgely would remain forever lit.

A group of good old boys gather at Buckley Wellington's home every Saturday to watch the Wolverines battle it out on the grid- iron. The TV has performed flawlessly since the installation of Jock Jeffers, whose record string of interceptions was cut short when he got creamed by five of Cornell's meatiest players. Jock is now tuned in to reception of a different kind.

Buoys will be buoys unless they're lucky enough to be stuffed preppies. Known for their buoyant spirits on land and on sea, Hobart Applegate and Farley Carruthers proved less than unsinkable when they listed too far to port while tacking into Hobe Sound. Now their bells ring out "My Bunny Lies Over the Ocean" as they guide parched skippers back to the yacht club bar.

None of his classmates at U. Va. boasted a collection of Lacoste shirts that could parallel that of Peabody Lindquist, Jr. When Peabody's Porsche missed a crucial curve one night after a road trip to Sweet Briar, it was deemed fitting that he be sent in to protect baby gators from their age-old enemy, the predatory wood stork. Peabody's buddies were scared shirtless at the thought that the little reptiles might someday be extinct.

Bootsie Buxton's ballet teacher never imagined that her star pupil would take her literally when she instructed the dainty ballerina to do a split. But luckily it was a clean break, and Bootsie was taped back together again in perfect balance. Now her fellow ballet students belly up to Bootsie as they toe the mark. Even though Bootsie had never carried such weight in class before, she makes a wonderful barrebelle.

Happy-go-lucky Beresford Taylor had always taken to water like a duck, so it came as a ghastly surprise to his loved ones that the distance between Nantucket and the Vineyard was beyond his breaststroke. Sucked under by a remorseless undertow, Berry was later planted heels up, and the family beach umbrella became his sole responsibility.

*R*ealizing it was the prepski thing to do, Parker Dillingsworth didn't feel at all guilty when he quit the slopes at noon to relish some heavy après-ski action. A dozen hot-buttered rums later, Parker staggered out to his BMW, but failed to locate the ignition. He spent that night in sub-zero temperatures, and the rest of his nights racked-out as never before.

Conceited Gretchen Goosedown didn't know that pride went before a fall until she took a vicious spill on the third hurdle at the Radnor Hunt Club. Her parents decided it would be too cruel to separate their darling from the stable she loved, so Gretchen was transferred from hoof to roof and left there, whether vain or not.

Each year when spring vacation rolls around, New York City swells with thirsty preppies, and nowhere is the tapping of Top-Siders more pleasing than at Swell's, where the annual Mount Gay and Coke-drinking marathon is a mecca for all the big barfers and heavy heavers from Exeter to Woodberry Forest. In fact, by the end of last year's gala, four of the participants had tossed their last cookies, but their heads will spin through many a future contest.

It simply didn't occur to Pendergast Putnam that the bar car was the last one on the 5:02, and a graceful, if unintentional, exit to the rear left him sprawled on the third rail midway home. Having made his last three-martini commute, Pendy will never again get his signals crossed.

It seemed much the easier way for the Wittinghams to donate a bench to the Princeton stadium in memory of their son, Spence. Bloated from excess beer intake during his days as a Tiger, Spence stretches out as a soft, if stiff, seat for the roaring home team.

Having the misfortune of teeing off at Burning Tree just ahead of a former high-ranking government official named Ford, Geoff Sutton was discovered in the rough three days later with a golf ball embedded in his forehead. The first of his set to be stuffed with woods and irons, Geoff caused the links crowd to wonder why a preppy had never before been recast as a golf bag. All it took was a hole in one.

It was just too embarrassing for Bambi Bancroft when she couldn't, in all of St. Louis, find an escort for the Veiled Prophet Ball. Bambi begged Mummy to solve this ickypoo dilemma, and Mummy dug up Thornton Van Rensselaer, who the weekend before had fox-trotted into the deep end of the pool after a liquid evening at the Ladue Country Club, when he couldn't have held his own even in the shallow end. Wrung out and wound up for a waltz, Thorny indeed provided the key to solving Bambi's problem.

When indulging in an evening to the max, Muffy Woodruff would intermittently leap upon a table at P.J. Clarke's to make like a Rockette. The good times ran out when Muffy's foot overturned an unopened bottle of Dom Perignon. The cork was ejected with truly murderous force, catching Muffy in the navel. Through her escapades, she had become such a part of the ambiance that her bubbly personality couldn't be totally removed. The only bother was in having to explain to curious customers how Muffy had kicked the bucket.

The evening was to die...the bartender at Nini Saltmarsh's deb party at the Plaza was pouring triples, and Oliver Oglethorpe III fancied it would be a hoot to crown the event with a little fountain jumping. Oblivious to the fact that the fountain had been drained for repairs, Oliver plunged in with panache. Later the gang made certain that he came to a splashy end anyway and that he would never dry out.

Reeves Talmadge, who had a reputation for telling tall tales, had barely left Daddy's hunting lodge when he received a not so affectionate bear hug from a furry, sharp-toothed creature who took him from behind. Hug led to rug, and now Reeves lies without reproach.

The supposed managerial skills of fraternity presidents make them attractive to corporate headhunters, but these four, having soaked their brains in beer for four years, were found wanting on Wall Street. They were shipped back to Psi U where, as in jollier days, they became quite hung up on themselves.

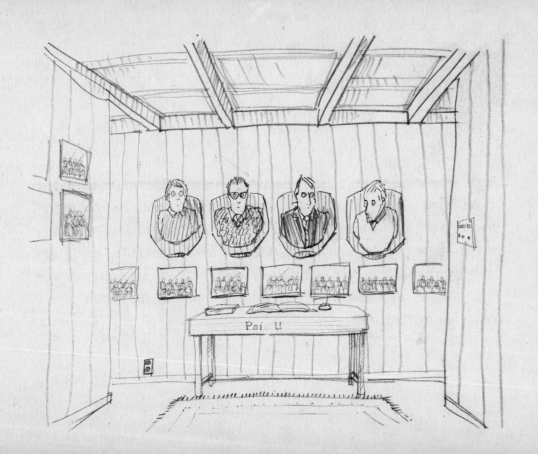

The Heppenstalls and the Crestwoods were considered pillars of the Greenwich community, and it was a dreadful loss to society when their golf carts collided head-on at the tenth tee one foggy July morning. Despite the catastrophe, not an unsightly bruise was visible, and the four were able to continue supporting their beloved country club.

*D*uring his last spring vacation from Dartmouth, Proctor Witherspoon IV took a miscalculated turn onto a sinister cork-screw trail and in no time at all discovered why Jackson Hole is so named. Since skiing had always given him a lift, Proctor was allowed to travel round and round every winter thereafter, reaching out with a T for two.

Libby Hartley abstained from picking up her room for an unhealthy length of time and in March disappeared in the debris, choking on turtlenecks, Fair Isle sweaters, and wraparound skirts. Thanks to Muriel, who came in three times a week, Libby was plugged in and ultimately made a clean sweep of things with her Locust Valley lockjaw.

NEW YORKER

Since Chumley's bark was always worse than his sight, his owner Chet Breckinridge wasn't the least bit surprised when the Lab bounded noisily into a puddle of quicksand. Heartbroken at the thought of hunting without his best chum, Chet had him stuffed into a portable pal who, strictly speaking, no longer qualified as a retriever, being a pointer of no return.

Clayton Griswold and Cameron Sheffield caught a wild oar in the ear while rowing on the Charles one misty morning, and Harvard lost two stellar crewmen to the hungry river. Not willing to shell out big bucks for new racks, the coach applied several coats of varnish to Clay and Cam. They were named honorary members of the team, but were situated within the boathouse because the others couldn't stand to see any of their crew cut.

*W*hen but a trembling deb, Bitsy Butterworth swore she would never miss a regatta. So after the boom struck her once too often in a nasty squall off Edgartown, she was refitted in a forward-looking fashion, her shocking-pink espadrilles pointing the way to Hyannis Port.

Jamie Howells cut in on Morgan Stockwell one too many times during the last dance of the summer. Amanda Wagner, the object of their attention, suggested a sailing duel to settle the dispute. She insisted on overseeing the contest from a third boat, but, like the boys, overlooked a jagged jetty buried in a fogbank. The boats were lost, but not the remains of the trio, who, when not flying Old Glory, can do pennants for their fatally sloppy sailing.

Although she didn't bow to astrological fads of the day, Gilly Stanhope reveled in her Sagittarian birth after meeting an archer who gave her quivers. But his love was not steadfast . . . nor was his right hand, which one day released an arrow prematurely, making Gilly the target of his inattention in one too many ways.

The summer that Marshall Frawley decided not to keep off the grass was the season he was mowed down by a high fever. Now a head-shop fixture, Marshall is stiffer in the joints than ever before and makes no bones about being one toke over the line.

The Babcock brothers were always first — first onto the tennis court, first up to the beer keg, first every day into the family's Olympic-sized pool. When each tried to be first behind the wheel of Daddy's new BMW, the brawl that ensued was first-rate, and brought about the end of all three. Afterward, Mummy and Daddy reforged the links between their boys, but no longer were they leaders. They were a trailer.

Several of the mares at The Madeira School are unpredictable mounts, and at times dislodge their riders by cantering under low-hanging branches. Stunned girls thus hurtle on to greener and pinker pastures while their sophisticated veneers remain behind, keeping one jump ahead of the horses.

Dudley Thornhill decided to go for it when his brother bet him a case of brewski that he wouldn't jump off the chair lift at Stratton. Having a case and a half under his belt, Dudley didn't think twice and sailed through the air onto an icy boulder beneath. Beerless and still fearless, he now points the way to a somewhat less risky route down.

EXPERT ⚠

Sheridan Pendleton enjoyed the reputation of big swordsman on the Duke campus, but his reign ended abruptly when foiled in his attempt to woo a Delta Gamma, whose boyfriend took exception —and rapier—to his rival. Sheridan never recovered from that lunge and thrust, but re-armed and donated to the art department, he embodies the very model of propriety.

*D*addy wanted to throw Margot Whitney a coming-out party unlike any Darien had ever witnessed, but the market took such a tumble that he was forced to cut expenses dreadfully. His Lester Lanin look-alikes were actually vodka victims from past deb balls. Margot's Victrola did all the work. No guest was any the wiser until the needle stuck in a swinging rendition of "Chattanooga Choo Choo" and the evening ended abruptly when everyone realized there was no conductor.

A group of renowned revelers, the members of the class of '71 displayed little temperance when they returned to St. Paul's for their tenth reunion. Heeding the call of Turkey Pond, four ripped reunionites decided to take a midnight dip and opted for the course of least resistance when the choice came to swim or sink. The balance of the class recognized a practical — and economical — reunion gift to the school, and the departed shortly became the most upright of their peers.

It was a sad day when the St. Lawrence soccer team and accompanying cheerleaders were wiped out on the field by a flash flood, but happily their lower extremities were not long without the security of Top-Siders. Before the water had entirely receded, an entrepreneurial freshman gathered the remains and shrewdly created a market for athletes' feet.

When his ball bounced to within six inches of an unfriendly rattler, a hazard with which he was unfamiliar, Trip Llewellyn was not dismayed. But before he could swing his club, the serpent struck, and the duffer bit the dust. Brushed-up and positioned with his mouth still open in surprise, once dim-witted Trip is now forever on the ball.

Arch rivals for the position of goalie on Dana Hall's varsity field hockey team, Topsy Armstrong and Pookie Armbruster finally had it out minutes before the Concord Academy game. After each had achieved her goal of eliminating the competition, their crafty coach contrived a final standoff between the two.

Impish Stanton Fairfax persuaded a pair of freshmen to get their rears in gear and go mooning one starless night. Gripped by the desire to flash a buttock or two himself, Stanton, at the wheel, plowed the Country Squire into an Andover haberdashery. The less than clever lads were restyled as dummies and were rotated to face the window, leaving all aspects of their asinine behavior behind them.

Days before graduation from Middlesex, Dexter Trimingham and Thatcher Randolph found themselves on the wrong side of paradise when caught with the rye in the library stacks. Making good his pledge that no boy would leave school alive if found smashed, the headmaster subsequently made use of them, and each became a separate piece of the bookcase in their old dorm room.

Never ones to let boredom set in, Wiley Kimball and Biff Billingsworth decided it would be a stitch and a half to windsurf off Block Island during Hurricane Agnes. Bored they weren't, until two woodworkers fixed what the breakers had broken and rendered the daring duo seaworthy once more.

Lindsay Littlefield never strayed too far from the bar at any social gathering. Indeed, it seems this was the safest spot for her. For one evening, in search of the powder room, she strolled off a fifth-floor terrace at the University Club. It was decided that Lindsay's top third would stack up well against any ice chest.

Bixby Rutherford's macho mannerisms tended to offend even the most devoted debs. As he was crawling back to his rented cottage in the Hamptons early one August morning, the old sport's liver finally gave out. No longer does anyone mind when Bixby stands up for the male.

Vain to the point of blindness, the Calisher cousins refused to don specs — even horn-rims — until they pranced into Third Avenue one night after last call at the Ravelled Sleave. They were looking for a taxi, but one took them from behind before they caught sight of it. Heads intact, the three were poised to caution against the dangers of shortsightedness.

*D*orsey Beddington's penchant for falling asleep before going home was to be his downfall for, during one blowout, he nodded off on Missy Turner's bunk and was buried under a fatal quantity of field coats and Burberrys. The gear looked so suitable on his rigid, supine form that he was upended and placed in a more decorous surround at the University Club where, at last, his arms were coated rather than his tongue.

The one thing preppies weren't prepped for was extinction, but one black day beer ran dry, ducks winged away, Top-Siders turned bottoms up, and Fishers Island crumbled into the sea. It got even worse: Family trees withered at the root, old boy networks shorted out, and signet rings crested. The finest specimens of the subspecies (preppagundis Americus) *were then stuffed and allocated to the most prestigious of natural history museums. And strange to tell, life went on, but without that distinct* esprit de corps, *that* je ne sais quoi *that preppies had showered for centuries on the rest of the world far beneath them.*

PREPPAGUNDIS.
AMERICUS